LEARN TO THINK LIKE AN ENTREPRENEUR
AND CHANGE YOUR LIFE

TORTOISE
WALKING
FOR BEGINNERS

IAIN SCOTT

For Clair, Rosie and Adam

First Published in Great Britain by Enterprise Island

Enterprise Eilan Limited, Registered Office, 6 Belgrave Terrace,
Glasgow, G12 8JD

www.enterpriseisland.com

First Published 2004

ISBN 0-393-9743-4

A CIP catalogue record for this book is available from the British Library.

Set in Goudy Oldstyle
Photographs by Justine Lester **www.jlphotographic.com**
Designed and typeset by John McHugh, Glasgow **www.maganga.com**
Printed and bound by Creative Colour Bureau, Glasgow

introduction

The problem with every single business start-up book I have ever read is, they all tell you that you need to have a business plan before you can start a business.

Then they show you what a business plan looks like and it's at that point that 99.9 per cent of the people who have picked up the book in the hope of finding out how to start a business, decide that if starting a business is all about writing down turnover forecasts and growth projections, then it's not for them. They would rather stay in a job they hate, go on the dole, forget the dream they had . . . anything rather than start up a business because it's obviously just too scary and soul destroying and not for the likes of them because they're not Richard Branson.

Believe me - those books lie.

Many successful businesses are not started on the back of a business plan. One successful entrepreneur told me recently, "I wouldn't recognise a business plan if it jumped up and bit me on the nose." The conventional business plan comes way down the list of things to do - or not to do - before you're ready to start up a business. The truth is, every successful business starts, not with a business plan but with a conversation. It might be a conversation with yourself or somebody else or with a group of people and it usually goes along the lines of, "Wouldn't it be good to . . ." or "What this place really needs is . . ." or "I had this idea and I wondered if ... ". And, of course, there are the conversations that start: "I can't stick this job anymore . . ." or "I can't find work anywhere - how am I going to earn a living?"

Tortoise Walking for Beginners, then, is like no other business start-up book you have ever read.

It is based on the premise that conventional business plans are optional and that, furthermore, anyone can learn to become an entrepreneur and start a business (yes - anyone; even you cowering in the corner over there!). If you have ever had the faintest stirring of a desire to start up a business, this book is for you.

Not only does TWFB refuse to worship at the altar of the great god Business Plan, it also recognises that the journey - and it is a journey - to "destination entrepreneur" is a voyage of discovery. And it's a voyage of discovery that, even if you ultimately decide that entrepreneurship is not for you, will have a positive and lasting impact on your life.

So fellow tortoise walkers, I hope you enjoy the journey.

[signature]

P.S.   The story of how this book came to be called "Tortoise Walking for Beginners" is already the subject of various myths, legends and downright lies. Discover the truth by logging onto the Enterprise Island website (www.enterpriseisland.com). And please - feel free to add your own, entrepreneurial interpretation to the story.

P.P.S.   I would like to assure readers that no tortoises were harmed in the production of this book.

Tortoise Walking For Beginners is presented in three distinct parts.

Part One is about Talking Things Through and comes from my central thesis that enterprise and business are social activities. The reason many of us don't start enterprises is because we have nobody to talk to about our ideas and we're frightened of talking about them. So Part One is a technique to help you change your outlook and start the process of becoming a more enterprising person.

Part Two moves you a bit further on your journey. Most of us never find out how truly enterprising we actually are, yet we all have a huge range of enterprising skills and abilities. Over the last 15 years, I've drawn on characteristics identified by the American academic, J.G.Birch as being those most commonly associated with enterprising people. What I've done in TWFB is incorporate those characteristics into a series of questions to help you identify your enterprising abilities. This element will build your confidence and give you greater self-knowledge. As a result, you will then be able to progress to Part Three which is about doing it - taking the leap and starting that business.

Part Three comprises 20 of the questions that would-be entrepreneurs are most frequently asked by other entrepreneurs and that brings us right back to the starting point of this book which is that every good business starts with a conversation. Nobody funds (or backs or buys into) a business plan - they fund the person that wrote it. That's why I've called this section The Alternative Business Plan because you will see no mention of finance, marketing and growth projections. What you will get are the 20 key points that go into assessing what makes a successful entrepreneur.

PARTONE
TALKING THINGS THROUGH

I didn't know I was an entrepreneur.

I had a traditional Scottish education where you more or less did what you were told. Then I went to university, studied history and, when I left, had the option of doing two things: to go into arts management - which fell through - or teaching. Never did I consider starting a business; it just wasn't on the agenda. I enjoyed my teaching but after five years I packed it in, went on a business start-up course, cashed in my pension and started my first business. How did that happen?

In retrospect - having worked with hundreds of would-be entrepreneurs since then - I realise that, without being aware of it, I had gone though the essential process of Talking Things Through. If you want to become an entrepreneur, the first thing you have to do is say: "I want to become an entrepreneur. I want to start my own business." And when you've got that out of the way - and it's one of the most liberating things you can do - you can start Talking Things Through. It can be difficult at first. I started doing it by saying: "I'm not happy at work." To begin with, I said it to myself and then it came out as a bit of a whinge to my wife and then, a while later, as a bit of a whinge to some of my colleagues.

An interest for me at the time was cooking and I was finding it incredibly annoying that you couldn't get good quality food - because this was Scotland in the early 1980s. There were additives in everything and the range and the variety of food was pathetic. I started experimenting with traditional British dishes, which I then gave to friends to try out. Their response was so positive that I started talking about the whole idea of making food for people to buy. At this stage, I still didn't believe that I was going to start a business. I was just going to do something that I thought was quite good and could earn some money.

But I began to ask lots of people for their views on what I was planning to offer - dishes like Sussex Braised Steak and Rumbledethumps, which is an old Scottish recipe. I asked them what it was that they wanted in the way of food because it was the start of the era of 'work/life balance' with more people working longer hours and wanting better, ready-made meals because they didn't have time to cook for themselves. And I began to draw that information out of people simply by talking to them and listening to what they had to say. What I learned was that, yes, people would pay money for good quality food; that they wanted to be able to microwave it - because that was just beginning to take off - and they also wanted home delivery.

Now, you could call that Market Research but I prefer to call it

"There is only one way to make a great deal of money; and that is in a business of your own."

J. Paul Getty,
Former oil tycoon and once the richest man in America

Talking Things Through because by using the Talking Things Through method, I not only got lots of essential information from people, I also got confidence in myself - confidence that I wasn't an idiot and that my idea wasn't stupid - which is equally important in the process of becoming an entrepreneur. Once you've gone over the first hurdle of announcing: "I want to become an entrepreneur. I want to start a business", you've actually begun the journey of starting your own business.

What will happen next is, people will respond to your announcement in one of two ways. Some people will say: "That's really good!" and others will say: "You? Start a business?" But whichever way they respond, it will make you start looking at what it is you're planning to do and why you want to do it. Talking Things Through is a two level process. First, you're finding out about an idea that you've had. We know that every minute of the day, somebody has a business idea but they don't usually do anything about it. They just leave it. So by talking the business idea through - and by continuing to talk and to listen - you're gathering information.

A good example of this is the story of a couple who were on holiday in America where they came across a very efficient electronic midge repeller. When they got back to Scotland - which is awash with midges - they started talking about it very enthusiastically to a friend who said: "What a fantastic idea! Why didn't you bring some back with you?" They ended up importing

> "What I know is, that if you do work that you love, and the work fulfils you, the rest will come."
>
> **Oprah Winfrey**

a whole pile of them and selling them here. In effect, they started a business within a matter of weeks. How did that happen? Almost without realising it, the couple had started Talking Things Through with a friend whose response had been: "Fantastic idea . . . I know lots of people who would buy one."

Of course, not every business is set up as easily as that. For many of us, the Talking Things Through process takes more time. Another entrepreneur I worked with started off by saying he wanted to make crazy garden gnomes but ended up opening a coffee shop. How did that happen? He had begun by discussing his original idea with a group of friends and that led on to a general discussion about what was missing in their own lives and that, in turn, led them to the realisation that the one major thing that was missing in the small town they lived in was a good coffee shop. But the other thing that had also been happening while he was talking his idea through, was that his confidence was building. When you say you're going to start a business and you start Talking Things Through, you've put yourself on the line. Saying you're going to start a business is the hardest part of starting it up.

The second level of the Talking Things Through process concerns how people respond to a declaration that someone intends to start a business. How people around you respond to that

"In business there are no rules - morality yes, but rules never."
Iain Scott

has, more often than not, got a lot to do with the culture you are living in. I should point out, before we go any further, that I believe entrepreneurs are made - not born. Yes, there always have and always will be people who seem to have been born with the business gene - they just go out there and do it. But by and large, it's something you learn how to do. And you can learn to do it at 7, 17, 27 or 70. How quickly you learn how to do it and whether you ultimately set up a business will largely depend on how people react to your idea as you embark on the Talking Things Through process.

If somebody has been telling you all the time that you're fat and ugly, ultimately you will believe that you are fat and ugly. If somebody tells you that you can't do something, you'll ultimately believe that you can't do something. But it is equally the case that if somebody tells you that you can be an entrepreneur, you will believe it. So it's extremely important that when Talking Things Through, you do it with sensible, positive people. There is a place for people who say: "You're not going to do it." But your response to that - and this is a useful exercise for you to carry out - is to say "Why not?" What generally happens when we come up with an idea and somebody knocks it down is that we don't challenge them. But we should. If you say: "I'm going to open a coffee shop," and somebody tells you it's a stupid idea, ask them why. And listen to what they tell you because built in to Talking Things Through is the need to listen. By listening, you'll begin to become a much better judge of people and to be able to decide whose judgment you value.

"The only place where success comes before work is in the dictionary."

Vidal Sassoon
entrepreneur

I remember going to a conference where somebody stood up and said: "It's taken me 25 years but I've finally got myself into a position where I refuse to listen to people that I don't like or work with people that I don't like." Now, you may be thinking that it's easier to say something like that than to actually do it but what he went on to explain was that 70 per cent of his colleagues were negative and it was pulling him down so now he only worked with the thirty per cent who were positive - and he's improved so much more in what he's doing.

When I first started researching entrepreneurship, I interviewed an amazing woman who had taken on a catering franchise. When I asked her what had made her start a business, she replied: "Well, I couldn't have done it if I hadn't divorced my husband first." Then she explained: " I wasn't happy with my life and when I looked at what I was doing, I realised that I had the potential, the skills and the ambition to run my own business. When I asked myself what was stopping me, the answer was - my husband. I knew then that I wasn't going to be able to achieve what I was capable of until he was out of the picture. So I divorced him. Then I was able to start my business and focus all my energies on that. I'm now happily married again to someone who really supports what I'm doing."

I'm not suggesting that everyone who wants to start a business should get a divorce first! But that story illustrates what I've been saying about Talking Things Through and how it is a way of not

"Personally I aim for maximum margin, minimum effort. After all, you want to enjoy life."
Iain Scott

only gathering information about what you want to do but also of learning how you're going to get to the point where you can do it. When you tell people you're going to start a business, watch their reactions. Learn from them, listen to them and challenge them as well. If someone says your idea is rubbish, go through the exercise of asking them why and you'll find that, not only will you be gathering market information you will, more importantly, be building up a core of strength in your own abilities.

Learning in this way, by Talking Things Through, doesn't come naturally to everyone - me included. I had a very good education but, in the traditional way, it was focused on analysis. At school, I studied English, Maths, Latin and so on all from books, of course. I then compounded that by going on to university to do History. I had a fabulous time there and learned many great skills but what I didn't learn to do was trust my own judgment. For everything we needed to know, we turned to books. Typically, when I decided to start my own business, I went on a course because that was the 'right' way to do it. That's the way we were told it was done. Nothing taught me to trust my own judgment. In the run up to starting my own business, I was heavily influenced by other people, some who gave good advice, some who gave bad advice and some who gave advice when they weren't in a position to give advice at all.

"Entrepreneurs capitalise on chaos!"
David McKnight

And that's the other danger you'll encounter when you're starting your own business. You're always up against people who've got an opinion but no experience and no actual advice to offer. True entrepreneurs are always very happy to give advice and while some of them are highly opinionated people, there is a difference - their opinions are based on experience. The funny thing about most entrepreneurs is, if you disagree with them, they really like it because you're challenging them and they like that challenge.

People who want to start businesses don't always know, at the beginning, exactly the kind of business they want to start up. If you're in that situation, just pluck any idea out of the air that appeals to you and watch the reaction when you say, for instance, that you want to make blow up plastic dolls. I've continued to do that since starting my first business and because of that, I've been accused of being a professional troublemaker! But that's not why I do it. When I get an interesting idea, I like to get feedback from people and I throw it out to them. Entrepreneurs always have ideas and some people find ideas threatening - especially if they're unusual ones. One participant on my Enterprise Island Challenge had designed and made a beautiful leather teddy bear, which she took along to a business advisor. Instead of telling her that it was a fantastic product and that she should go for it and take her idea on to the next stage, he said: "What happens if one of the people involved in manufacturing the bears for you leaves a needle in one of them by accident . . ." and he then went on to list around 20

"It may be a cliché but people invest in people."
Darren Smith

different Health and Safety problems that could crop up, almost killing the idea and her enthusiasm stone dead in the process. Fortunately, she bounced back. Although the business advisor may have had a point that was not the time to bring it up. I'm not recommending that you plunge straight in, put your house on the line and sell all your possessions just to go and make leather teddy bears. Neither am I saying that you should ditch your husband before you start a business! But when you start telling people you're going to set up a business, and when you start going through the Talking Things Through process and get a negative response, put the ball back in their court. Ask them why you shouldn't become an entrepreneur and set up a particular business and in that way, you'll find out where they're coming from.

There has been a lot of research done which indicates that people who talk things through suffer less stress than people who internalise things and bottle them up. So your first step to becoming an entrepreneur is to say: "I'm going to start a business." Then watch people's reactions. Assess how they respond to your idea and listen to what they say. Then go out and do it again and keep on doing it in a continuous cycle: talk, listen, reflect, act. Talk, listen, reflect, act. Talk, listen, reflect, act; assessing all the time how people respond to you and what they say.

Up in the Highlands in Scotland there is a fabulous conference centre, which is the only large size amenity of its kind in the area. When the hotelier who built it went to a market research advisor

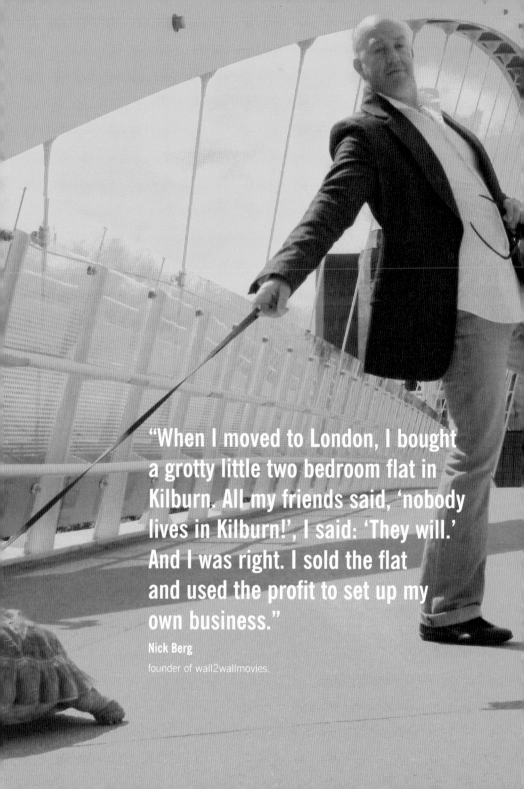

"When I moved to London, I bought a grotty little two bedroom flat in Kilburn. All my friends said, 'nobody lives in Kilburn!', I said: 'They will.' And I was right. I sold the flat and used the profit to set up my own business."

Nick Berg
founder of wall2wallmovies.

with the idea they told him not to do it. But he thought: "I know this area inside out, I know lots of business people and I know they haven't got anyplace to meet. Added to which, I've got a good reputation as a hotelier so I'm just going to build this thing anyway." Which he did and it's been a phenomenal success. But the reason he's getting the business is because, rather than open a bog standard conference centre, he built a superior one, offering good food and good service.

Let's take Ben and Jerry's Ice Cream as another example of that kind of thing. Here were two entrepreneurs who said: "We're going to make ice cream that's going to be top notch quality with the best ingredients and an ethical policy." And people told them it would never work. How wrong they were! And they said the same thing to Anita Roddick. But both of these highly successful companies were started by people who had Talked Things Through. When you Talk Things Through, you're meeting your future customers and you're getting information and inspiration; what I call the two 'ii's. You will also get some negativity but if you can handle that negativity, you're on to the next stage of becoming a successful entrepreneur. If people are being negative and saying no, does that mean your idea isn't a good one? Not necessarily. If someone says 'no' to you, ask them why. Don't listen to the 'no', listen to the reason behind the 'no'. Don't be afraid to ask. What's wrong with asking? How bad is 'no'? 'No' is just part of the way to 'yes'! As soon as you tell somebody that you're going to start a business, the process has begun - the meter is running. You don't have to say

"If it was easier for people to start up businesses, everybody would be doing it! Obstacles make life more interesting and exciting."

George Kinghorn
serial entrepreneur.

what that business is and it doesn't matter who you tell. It could be your nearest and dearest - or a complete stranger. The next time you're at a party and somebody asks you what you do, say: "I'm just about to start my own business." And watch the reaction. What you've said will either be a conversation stopper or a conversation opener. But my bet is on the opener. In my experience, every time you tell somebody you're going to start a business, their usual response is: "My God, you're giving up your job! You're so brave!" And don't be surprised if they also add: "I've always wanted to do that myself." Then go find another individual and repeat the process. You'll be amazed at how interested people are in what you're going to do. Then watch the reaction as other people round about you hear what you plan to do. It's a bit like a pebble in a pond!

If you're married or in a steady relationship, you've got to say to your partner at the earliest opportunity that you're thinking of starting a business.

It mustn't come as a complete bolt from the blue. But judge what the reactions are going to be because there will be worries. They might assume, for instance, that it means you're packing in your job immediately and that a large part - or even all - of the family income will stop. So when you're Talking Things Through, tease out other people's fears because they will have fears, for themselves and for you. And you'll have fears for yourself as well. Don't just say: "I'm going to start a business" and then, if they reply with: "I don't think you should" respond by saying that you're going to do

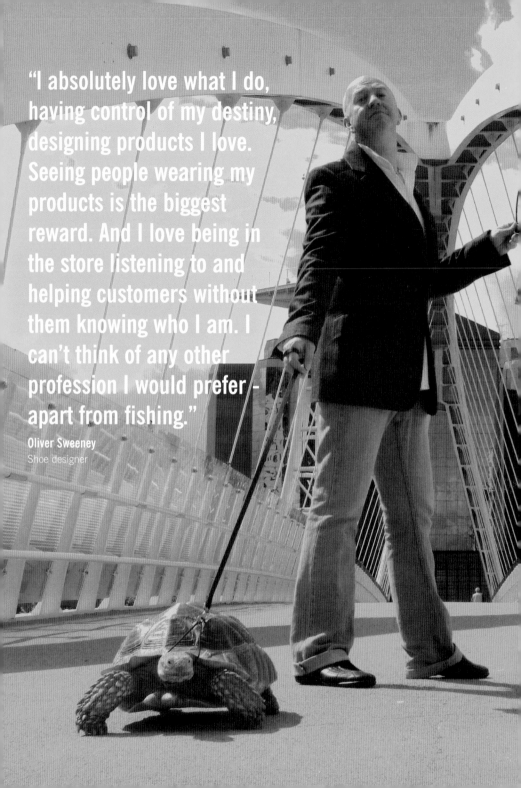

"I absolutely love what I do, having control of my destiny, designing products I love. Seeing people wearing my products is the biggest reward. And I love being in the store listening to and helping customers without them knowing who I am. I can't think of any other profession I would prefer - apart from fishing."

Oliver Sweeney
Shoe designer

it anyway. If your partner says they don't think you should start a business, don't have a fight about it. Ask them why. They might be worried that starting a business means the mortgage won't get paid. In which case, your response might be: "You don't need to worry about that because I'm not going to go into business full time. I'm keeping on my job and I'll build up the business and see how it goes."

Get your partner to write down their worries about what starting a business might mean and then go through them together because if you can address those worries in a calm, considered way, you'll be better equipped to run a more successful business. Contrary to what most people think, entrepreneurs don't take risks - they take calculated risks. Talking Things Through is the way to calculate those risks. When I started my first business, I spoke to 30 or 40 people. I said I was thinking of making high quality food and one of the people I spoke to had a shop. Her advice was to open a factory because she had become disenchanted with retail. Somebody else I spoke to told me about the various grants that were available to people setting up a food business. Then I went and spoke to someone at Harrods, told them I was making high-quality gourmet meals and they said: "Excellent! Let's taste them." They thought they were fantastic and Harrods became one of my first customers. In Glasgow, I took one of the cakes I was making to the owner of a chain of delis where the owner said:

"We've got lots of cakes already and we don't need any more." But I persuaded him to taste mine and he said: "Oh, that's really

"Starting a business is a financial and professional commitment. But even more, it is an emotional one."

Mark McCormack
International sports agent.

good!" and I replied, "So I take it we're in business?" and he said: "Oh, all right then!" So I had another customer.

Although you might start off expecting a lot of negative reaction, you will be pleasantly surprised at how positive many people will be. And that's one of the exciting things about starting a business. Once you've committed yourself to doing it, go out and talk to someone every day about what you're going to do. Never stop talking, never stop listening and never stop thinking. You may not start your business immediately. If there are family issues and personal issues to deal with, you may have to put it on hold. It may not happen for several years. But once you've said you're going to be an entrepreneur and start up your own business, there's no going back. You will do it eventually.

Talking Things Through means you have given yourself permission to start a business and you validate that as you go through the process. Only you can give yourself permission and the minute you say: "I'm going to start a business" you have done just that. I remember someone saying to me, shortly after I'd started my first business, that I'd do better if I wore a more sombre tie. If I was as confident then as I am now, I would have said that the type of tie I chose to wear had nothing whatsoever to do with how successful my business was going to be. But I didn't have the courage in those days - I was too polite. So I didn't say anything. What he meant, I suppose, was that you could only be successful if you were a boring, corporate pillock - which is what he obviously

"The entrepreneur is essentially a visualiser and an actualiser. They can visualise something and when they visualise it, they see exactly how to make it happen."

Robert Schwartz.

was. And maybe the business world was a bit like that 20 years ago. Times have changed, thank God and, now, it's never been easier to start a business in so many different areas. People can create a business from the strangest and most interesting ideas these days. And a lot of these businesses stem from trying to do what makes you happy. Look at Richard Branson. No one could say he hasn't enjoyed building up what has turned into one of the most successful businesses in the world. If you aren't enjoying what you're doing, why are you doing it? And beware those people who try to put a damper on your ideas and enthusiasm by asking if you've thought about how your team will be managed etc. Forget all of that.

Having given yourself permission to start a business, make sure you do it sensibly because you don't want to end up losing everything

including the shirt off your back. The message of this book is: everybody has the potential to start their own business. It may not be right for some people but everybody who has the desire to do so, can. Read the book and by the time you get to the end, you will be thinking and acting like an entrepreneur. If, ultimately, you decide that starting a business isn't for you, you will still have got something out of it. If your business lasts three hours, three days, three weeks, three years - or three generations - we want to make sure that your business works, that it works successfully and that, if it doesn't work, you come out of it undamaged.

PARTTWO
TESTING YOUR ENTERPRISING ABILITY

How do you test your enterprising ability?

A defining moment for me came when I was working up my first business. I'd already begun a home delivery service for my regional foods and the next stage was to make the big leap into full-time. To complement my original plan, I was looking at producing specialist cakes as well and I had made an appointment to discuss the idea with a business advisor with what was then the Scottish Development Agency Small Business Service - practising what I preach by Talking Things Through! Having explained to the business advisor what I planned to do, she looked at me and said: "You can't do that; somebody else is already doing the same thing." I said: "What do you mean, I can't do that?" And she replied: "I just told you - somebody else is already doing that so your business will fail."

I can still remember how absolutely furious I was. Who was she to tell me what to do? She didn't know me, she didn't know anything about me and there she was, this so-called business advisor; sitting behind her desk, on a salary, with a pension; there was I, on the other side of the desk, giving up a salary and a pension, making this big leap and having done a lot of work in the process. And it was at that point that I made the decision just to go for it and do what I wanted to do. That's when I really found my entrepreneurial ability.

Now, thinking back on that incident of some 20 odd years ago - and looking at the hundreds of people that I've worked with and helped - there's a pattern that emerges. So what we're going to do in this section is raise some of the issues and examine the things that will help you find out for yourself just how enterprising you are. It's a bit like a barometer. You can do a test now and a test later on. Firstly, start off the process by asking your friends: "Am I entrepreneurial?" That's because although you may not consider yourself enterprising, lots of other people might. See what the reaction is to the question and you may be pleasantly surprised.

My definition of an entrepreneur is somebody who makes something happen. They are ultimately 'do-ers'. Entrepreneurs are commonly assumed to be extrovert, full of bravado, big risk takers. This is not true. Entrepreneurs - really good entrepreneurs - assess the risks and ideally, they get somebody else to share the risks with them. But what really makes them different from other people is that, having reached the point where they've got the idea and the motivation, they actually do something about it. You'll have seen them in operation at work, in clubs and social situations. Based on my experience, I've drawn up a list of 10 questions, which will enable you to find out how enterprising you are. Read them through and answer them. Then rate yourself and get other people to do it for you.

Are you an optimist?

To answer that, start off by asking yourself: Is the glass half-full or half-empty? If you usually say that the glass is half-full then, clearly, you are an optimist. You look on the bright side of things. If, however, your answer is the glass is always half-empty, then I'm not convinced that starting a business is the thing for you. There are lots of ups and downs to starting a business and in order to get through those ups and down, you've got to have a spirit of optimism; you've got to have a bit of faith. Everybody gets knocks in this life but when you're starting a business and becoming an entrepreneur, you get continual knocks. If you don't have a bit of optimism about you, you will not see yourself through. You can go away and do something about it; you can turn yourself from being a pessimist into an optimist - but I'm not quite sure how!

Are you the sort of person who says: "I'll find a parking space" or are you the kind of person who says: "I'll never find a parking space - it will not happen." Entrepreneurs invariably find parking spaces, almost because they will them to appear. Being optimistic is not preparing yourself for disappointment because if you set out thinking you might fail, you will fail. You need to have the ability - and the charm - to persuade people to do things. An optimistic outlook is vital to the successful entrepreneur. If you refuse to accept 'no' for an answer, on the basis that 'something' will turn up, you eventually get what you want. Of course, you've got to be realistic and know when to cut your losses but, by and large, optimism is a wonderful gift.

QUESTION NUMBER TWO:
When you're doing something that you enjoy, do you work hard at it?

The expression 'time just flew by' fits in perfectly here because becoming an entrepreneur and starting your own business is hard work. So if you're not going to enjoy it, there's no point in doing it. Some people start up businesses that they end up not liking and life becomes miserable as a result. That doesn't mean they shouldn't have started the business in the first place. It just means it's time to get out and do something different. But ask yourself this question and answer it honestly: What do I like doing that I put my heart and soul into, that I willingly work unlimited hours at, during which time just flies by?

A workaholic is somebody who loves their work - all the time. It's not some 'saddo' who sits on the beach sending out business-related emails because they have to. It's someone who sits on the beach thinking about new ideas for a business and how much they're going to enjoy it. A workaholic gets pleasure from the work they do and delights in the fact that they're getting paid to do something they love doing. It's not like that all of the time but, most of the time, it is. However, it is true that there can be a danger in making a business out of the thing you love doing. You turn your hobby or your favourite pastime into a business and suddenly, you find you don't enjoy it anymore.

A useful tip that is given to people who say they'd love to run their own country pub is to work behind the bar of one of those pubs for just one day. If, at the end of the day, you're still keen, then that's a pretty good indication that you could run that kind of business. There is a big difference between sitting and enjoying a country pub atmosphere and being on the other side of the bar, serving. You'll need to be a naturally hospitable person who likes seeing other people having a good time, to get any pleasure from running a pub. But, oddly enough, the hospitality industry is a strange mix of people who adore what they're doing and others who hate it. To sum up: don't go into a business that you're not going to enjoy working at - most of the time!

QUESTION NUMBER THREE:
If you become involved in a project, do you like seeing it being done well?

From my experience, one of the things that entrepreneurs are good at doing is not only seeing a 'big picture' but also having an eye for the detail. The bits in between - the management side of things - are not what interests them. They have a vision and an eye for detail. It might be that little extra touch; the flowers on a table for a restaurateur for instance, or the quality of the book binding for somebody who is a publisher. They've just got that 'eye' and it makes what they're doing something special. If, however, you are the kind of person who tends to start projects and not see them through, that's a bit of a warning sign that you might not succeed as an entrepreneur. You've got to see a project through or at least know why you're 'killing' it. Good entrepreneurs, displaying good entrepreneurial behaviour, would say: "This is what I want to do, this is what I've got to do to get there and I will see it through."

It is true, of course, that sometimes a project has to be abandoned or at least shelved temporarily. Every entrepreneur has experienced the "I've got to get out of this fast, it's not worth the effort" moment. Things do not always go according to plan and projects have to be left. It may be that the time for your business wasn't right. There are lots of initiatives and projects out there that were ahead of their time. So along with all the other things you've got to pull together to get a business started, the market has got to be right and the idea has got to be right. The phrase: "an idea which was ahead of its time" is a useful one here because there's a point where you can have the funkiest cafe bar, but if the market isn't quite ready for it and you're too far ahead, then you'll really struggle. "An idea whose time has come", on the other hand, is just that fraction ahead of everybody else which means your funky cafe bar will have everyone saying: "Ooh - this is wonderful!"

Entrepreneurs don't let projects drift. They take command of the situation, they analyse it; they say: "What is it that we're going to do? Why do we want to do it? How are we going to get there?" If things aren't going according to plan, they then say: "I'm not achieving this because of X, Y and Z," and they then amend it to get it back on track and working they way they want it to.

Or they decide to leave it and move on to something else. But if they see that a project is going in the right direction but just requires a bit of 'kickass' to make it happen, then they kickass and make it happen! They don't sit back and say: "Oh well, it didn't really work out . . ." They go for it.

An entrepreneur has to be clinical and dispassionate at times. They have to be able to stand back from the situation and look at it objectively - even though they created it. Sometimes, they see a way to make an even better profit and a better return as they're going along. This can really confuse other people who have become involved in a particular project because, although entrepreneurs are good for ideas, they're not always very good at communicating their vision to others.

QUESTION NUMBER FOUR:
When you're getting involved in something, do you want it to be the best thing there is?

Are you passionate about what you are doing? If you're an entrepreneur - and a good entrepreneur - you will not accept second best. Think back on your life and think about something you have done. It might have been planning a wedding. Women have got fabulous skills yet the number of women who undersell themselves is phenomenal. Organising and planning a wedding, a birthday or any event calls for considerable skills. It requires good organisation, enthusiasm and commitment. It means seeing something through and having an eye for detail.

So if you're out there and you've just done a wedding - if you've organised it yourself - give yourself a pat on the back. You're an entrepreneur - you just didn't know it! When you're organising an event, there's no point in being luke warm. You've to have a bit of passion. If you get excited about things and you're passionate about them, you will communicate that to other people. The good thing about entrepreneurs is, they push other people along with their enthusiasm. But to become an entrepreneur, you have to recognise when other people are pulling you down. Which brings us to question number five.

QUESTION NUMBER FIVE:
'Control freak' or not?

Counter to expectations, entrepreneurs are not control freaks. They don't want to do everything themselves and they don't have to. That's because they are incredibly good at getting other people to do things for them. And they don't necessarily pay them! They may smile at them, do them a favour, etc. But they get people to do things for them by networking. What is networking? Networking is the art of going out and finding people who can help them get what they want. They speak to them, they talk to them, and they persuade them to come on board. Entrepreneurs build teams around them and they're very comfortable with that because they don't see any problems. They see somebody out there with a particular skill that they need to make things happen. Entrepreneurs can be very frustrating people to work for but they can also be very exciting people.

Ask yourself this: if a job needs doing, do you need to do it yourself? If you want to be an entrepreneur and you answered 'yes' to that, think again. Because feeling the need to do every job yourself is going to get in the way of you becoming an entrepreneur. It indicates that you have a tendency to become obsessive about particular points. The motto of the successful entrepreneur is: "If a job is worth doing, get somebody really good to do it." And if they don't do it well, sack them and hire someone else. That is the correct answer to that question.

A good analogy of that is the theatre producer. A theatre producer is the person who gets the whole show together: books the theatre, hires the cast, the director and the marketing people and then gets customers into the theatre. What gives the theatre producer a real 'high'? Seeing a theatre full of happy people - thoroughly enjoying drama, music, dance. Some producers are exceptionally skilled and can even do a bit of directing. But a really good producer is the person who makes it happen. It's magic. They are entrepreneurs. That's why the arts are full of entrepreneurial people. They have an amazing ability to conjure something out of nothing. But note that successful producers do not do everything themselves. They pick other people to do it for them. And when those other people do a good job, the good entrepreneur praises them for it because is a wonderful thing.

QUESTION NUMBER SIX:
Can you take responsibility?

Somehow, an entrepreneur takes responsibility. They say: "We're going to do this." They don't normally declare that they are going to take responsibility for a project, they just automatically assume it. They are natural leaders. It's unlikely that an entrepreneur would say: "We're going to do this and you will do as you are told." They get people on board through a combination of enthusiasm, motivation, eye for detail, organisational ability, etc. They take on responsibility for and take ownership of a project. It's a mother hen approach. It's to do with pride and wanting to do something well. They are behind the team - pushing people forward and taking a project forward.

If you've always been told that you couldn't organise anything, you probably believe it. The only way to overcome that is to go out and do something. Here's an analogy. The young child goes to wash its hands and the mother comes along and washes their hands for them, thereby taking away that child's sense of responsibility, pride and confidence - because somebody else will always do it for them. It's very constricting. And it's usually accompanied by: "Let me do this for you, you can't do it properly." But how difficult is it to wash your hands? If you don't do it yourself, you'll never learn. So mothers - step back from your children!

Ask yourself: Do I feel confident about taking on responsibility for a project? Ask yourself: Could I make it happen? And also ask yourself: If it goes wrong, how will I feel? Because entrepreneurs are not bothered by failure. This is where the Americans really score. Where entrepreneurship is concerned, they see failure as part of the learning curve. They say: "Well, I tried that but it didn't work so I moved on." I met an American recently who told me that she was selling a house she and her partner had bought just three years previously. It had land and stables for horses because they had wanted to experience the complete rustic lifestyle. And having experienced it, they decided it wasn't for them. So with no feelings of angst or sense of failure, they were selling up and moving back to the city to a modern high rise flat. In the UK, the reaction might have been: "we failed, the project didn't work, let's never try anything different again". In America they say: "we tried it, we didn't like it, let's move on". The American attitude is the responsible one. It's the entrepreneurial one. Taking responsibility does not mean taking the blame for something. It's just saying: "We tried this and it didn't work." But too often we equate responsibility with blame. We have a very strong consumer culture in this country which means that when there's a problem we say: "Who do we blame?" rather than: "How can we make it better?" If you're a 'blaming' person, you're going to find it difficult to be an entrepreneur. If you're non-judgmental, you'll find it easy to be an entrepreneur.

QUESTION NUMBER SEVEN:

Do you get upset when you've done something and done it well but few people acknowledge the work, effort and commitment you've put into it?

Now we're getting into your entrepreneurial ability and the process of becoming an entrepreneur. Because the process of becoming an entrepreneur is about saying to yourself: "Why am I working for this idiot? His office only runs because of me. I bring in all the work but my boss takes all the credit and all the money. I could do it for myself." Or: "Why am I working for these people? Why am I wasting my time playing office politics?" And if you get particularly upset when you aren't rewarded for the good work you do - then it's time to start your own business. In fact, before you go any further, write down all the things you are good at, then write down all the things you are weak at. Make up a balance sheet, look at it and ask yourself how other people would rate you. Then ask yourself if you get rewarded for any of the things you're good at.

QUESTION NUMBER EIGHT:
When you've done something, do you reward your achievement?

Sales people tend to live on rewards. If they've got a big sale, they want a reward. It might be a bottle of champagne, it might be a bonus. But they want a 'feel good' factor. Entrepreneurs are no different. If they've achieved something, they reward themselves. It could be a surf board (in my case!) but that's what keeps you going. Being able to treat yourself is one of the great things about being an entrepreneur. And when the going gets tough, give yourself a reward as well - for having got yourself through it.

QUESTION NUMBER NINE:
Do you have a desire to achieve?

Ask yourself: "What do I want out of life?" This book is dedicated to people who are on the journey to 'Destination Entrepreneur'. They want to become an entrepreneur and they want to start their own business. That may not, in the end, be right for everyone but it's part of the voyage of exploration and discovery. 'Desire to achieve' is not the same as being ambitious. Ambition is getting on and getting places. Desire to achieve is saying: "I want to change the way people look at a particular thing." Peter Wood, for example, when he started Direct Line, changed the way we look at insurance and that's a magnificent achievement. Anita Roddick wanted - and still wants - beauty without cruelty and a business with ethical policies. And wanting to achieve also ties in with, last but not least, money.

Contrary to popular belief, very few entrepreneurs start their business for money. The money is a means to an end. For some people it might be that they want to start a business which they can sell in five years' time and have the money to move to somewhere warm and sunny and have a good lifestyle. It might be property development. You start your business and by the time you're thirty you've made enough money to retire. Far from being unusual, you'd be surprised at the number of people who do just that. Entrepreneurs are not interested in money for its own sake. They're interested in what money can bring; a better life style, for instance, or a better education for their children. That's where the sense of achievement comes in.

QUESTION NUMBER TEN:

Once you've read all this and carried out the exercises, we come to the point where I say: "So why haven't you started your own business?" Which is question number 10. And what I want you to do now is write down six reasons why you haven't started it. And that's the starting point for actually making it happen.

PART**THREE**
MAKING THINGS HAPPEN

Nothing happens until somebody
sells something!

There is no point in selling
something unless you make a profit.

Do not confuse making a profit with
getting paid.

Remember these and you should not go wrong.

Traditionally, when someone is thinking of setting up a business, they're told that the first thing they should work on is the business plan. There are any number of books out there about how to write the perfect business plan. And I have to confess I found them useless. The reason for this is there are two types of business plan; one is a paper based exercise to help you secure funding and to persuade people that you know what you're talking about. The other is a useful tool to help you run a successful business. The problem for the majority of people starting out on their enterprise journey is that they don't know when the sales are going to come in, they don't know when they're going to get paid, they don't really know how much money they're going to make, so putting figures down on a bit of paper merely means you're put figures down on a bit of paper. It does not give you the real skills to get going.

I'm often accused of focussing on talking. But the one fundamental aspect of any successful entrepreneur is personality. People make businesses, not business plans. However, you have to be able to: one, sell your product and yourself; two, control the finances of your business; three, make sure it all happens. Just like tortoise walking, you never know what direction you're going to go in. What follows will help you, as the Americans put it, walk the talk.

The Alternative Business Plan.

The Alternative Business Plan comprises twenty questions that you should ask yourself and that other people will ask you. Traditional Business Plans are rigid - The Alternative Business Plan is about flexibility, keeping on your toes and making sure you are really focussed.

When I was a student studying History, one of the lecturers announced that he would explain how this wonderful subject helped to prepare us for life, by teaching us one important lesson. We waited with baited breath and the lesson was: "You never can tell." Over the years, starting businesses and working with other people starting businesses, I believe that the same applies to the world of the entrepreneur. Speak to any entrepreneur and they will tell you how what they thought was going to happen was not what eventually happened.

The problem with traditional business planning is that it suggests certainty. There is no certainty in business and you have to accept that. Running a business involves coping with change. Starting a business involves coping with change and chaos times ten! A cash flow forecast of anything longer than six months is useless.

To help you ensure you have the right attitude, you must be able to answer the following questions, and you must continue to answer these questions for the life of your business.

My aim is to ensure that you are now thinking like an entrepreneur!

GO ON SELL YOURSELF TO ME!

1. Who are you?

This is about selling yourself to me. I want to see, not a detailed CV with your academic achievements, but one that highlights what makes you tick. If you've been a mother looking after children for ten years, give me all the skills you've learned as a result. Convince me that if a problem occurs, you'll sort it out.

notes

SELL YOUR IDEA TO ME!

2. What are you selling?

Describe your product or service in no more than two sentences. Now, believe me, this is going to take you weeks because what people think they are going to be selling and what people think they are buying are two different things. Charles Revlon is reputed to have said: "I do not sell lipsticks, I sell smiles". If you're opening a hairdressing salon, in a street with four existing hairdressing salons, you will find it tough particularly if you sell hairdressing. But if you sell glamour or therapy and can charge a bit more for it, then you're on your way to being in business. This is one of the hardest aspects for any innovative business. Just think: bottled water is now a multi-billion pound industry. The concept in the UK was laughed at 20 years ago.

notes

3. What vehicle are you using to sell things?

For example: limited company, sole trader, and partnership. Do
not get hung up about this. This, in many respects, is a very
important part but it is not a priority. For if you have no sales, then
it doesn't really matter whether you're a limited company or a
partnership. I have a preference for limited companies. It
minimises risk - that's why the concept of limited liability was set
up. Some people prefer sole trade where you are the business and
the business is you. Then of course, there's the area of
partnerships. Once you have a clear idea of what you're selling, and
who you're selling to, then you should tackle this issue and get
specialist advice.

notes

4. Why will anyone buy your product or service?

Funny how it always comes back to sales. There's a tale of two fizzy drinks companies, one Coca Cola the other Pepsi. Why does Coca Cola sell more? Well, Pepsi would tell you that in blind tastes, their product is as good as, if not better than, the competition. So just because a product is good does not necessarily mean it will sell. What it comes down to is, how effectively you get people interested in what you're offering. This can be a catchy name, an image that captures people's imagination etc. but unless you go out and let people know your product is there, and ask them to buy it, you're not going to get anywhere. So in answer to this section, I would expect to see precisely how you're going to achieve those sales figures.

notes

5. How many people will buy your product?

Or to put it another way, how many units or services will you sell per year? Now, some people have it easy here. If you've been in the widget industry for ten years, you've got some pretty good inside information. You know when people buy, when they don't buy and what they're like and you've probably got a load of contacts. So you've got a head start here. If, on the other hand, you're trying something new (for example, when I made my frozen vegetarian meals, all the market research said vegetarianism was growing, and that there was a huge market for quality food that was well packaged. But none of it told me whether I would sell one, or one hundred, or a thousand.) You've got to be brutally honest with yourself. If you really don't know, you must keep your overheads really, really low because the more innovative the product, the greater the risk. There may be greater rewards, but you could have a very bumpy take-off.

notes

6. When will people buy your product or service?

In the hotel industry, they know that the week after New Year and Christmas is quiet. Accordingly, they amend the business. One tip I like to recommend is, take a calendar and block out the times when people will not buy your product.   This will give you a shape and an indication of how the business is going to go. This will also mean you've cut your overheads before the sales vanish as opposed to after.

notes

7. In what quantity will people buy your product or service?

Many years ago I invented a product for the Christmas market. It was a mince pie with a twist. We made our own pastry and our own mincemeat and it was generously enhanced with Macallan malt whisky. We called them Macallan Mince Pies and they were sold mail order through a very good company called Scottish Gourmet. Arthur Bell, the owner of the company, from his past experience, thought we would probably sell about 2000. We trebled that figure. Now the point of this story is, at least I knew I would be selling them from November to December and we had a rough idea, based on experience, of what we would sell but we greatly exceeded it. A nice outcome but it just goes to show, as anyone in business will tell you, when trying to predict sales, you never can tell.

notes

8. Go on - convince me you know your customers.

First of all a warning – I loathe market analysis. This is for the big companies. Remember - you're not a multi-national corporation. Your dealing with customers not markets. For example, if you run a hotel you should be able to do the Car Park Test i.e., tell me the style and quality of car that your customer will use. If it's top of the range BMWs, then I would imagine you're a pretty exclusive luxury hotel because that's what your BMW driving customers will want. This also means you will be advertising in pretty luxurious upmarket magazines. You will know what your customers read, what their likes and dislikes are. This is the kind of information I want from you. If you want, draw a picture.

notes

9. So - in a competitive world, why should I buy from you?

Just think of your last major purchase. Why did you choose A over B? Now - that's what people are going to be doing with you.

notes

PERSUADE ME THAT YOU KNOW HOW MANY BEANS MAKE FIVE!

This is the money section, which you have to get right for your own good and for the business's good. What I've done is created a simple set of questions, which you must be able to answer. They are designed to help you get a handle on the key figures necessary for the smooth running of your business.

10. What price will your product or service sell at (to the end customer)?

notes

11. What are the costs involved in making that product or service?

For example, if it's a cake, then flour, eggs, sugar etc. If it's a service, then it's your time.

notes

12. How much money will you make on that product or service?

So - this is the difference between 10 and 11. Cake sells at one pound: ingredients: 10 pence; you make 90 pence.

notes

13. What are you going to spend each month on rent, rates, heating, lighting, etc.?

These are your fixed costs. You should also include your labour costs here because even if you sell nothing, you'll still have to pay somebody. And you should certainly pay yourself. You may choose not to take that money but you must show that you are entitled to it.

notes

14. What additional costs are you likely to have?

For example, are you going to have a big advertising campaign?

notes

15. What costs will you incur which are one-off?

For example, a landlord may require that you pay a deposit. There might be decorating costs for an office. List those kinds of things.

notes

16. When will your first order come through the door?

notes

17. When will you get paid for that first order?

notes

18. When will your suppliers get paid?

notes

Now that you've answered these questions, you've entered the world of Cash Flow. Cash Flow is critical to a business because it represents the difference between the money going out the door on materials, suppliers, overheads etc. and money coming in the door. So if you sell a product in January for 10 pounds but you have to spend 5 pounds making it and delivering it and you don't get paid till February, you've got to find that 5 pounds or possibly more because you've got the next month's overheads coming in before you get paid in February. Ideally, you want to get paid before you spend anything. That's why a lot of mail order businesses are so successful.

CONVINCE ME!

The thing about a new business is, you never can tell what's going to happen. Think back to Part One when you learned to tortoise walk. It's about your skills and your ability to make decisions. Any investor will ultimately make their decision based on your ability to sort problems out and keep control. So in this final section, I want you to convince me that you've got what it takes.

19. What systems will you put in place to make sure that costs do not run away or get out of control?

For example, if you run a shop, how are you going to control shoplifting? These are the kinds of questions that people will ask.

notes

20. Last but not least, what makes you different or why should I back you?

Here goes - give it your all - I want precision, and I want passion.

notes

OVER TO YOU.

It's over to you. The subtitle of this book is: "Learn to think like an entrepreneur and change your life." That, I think, is what probably separates this book from just about every other other business start-up book.

Because I believe that enterprise does not start with a business idea - it starts with your state of mind. Every single book and programme about enterprise and start-up focusses on the business idea. But with every person I've ever worked with - either entrepreneur or aspiring entrepreneur - it hasn't been about the business idea. It's been about realising potential. And that's what Tortoise Walking For Beginners is all about. Tortoise Walking For Beginners is about helping you develop a different attitude; a new way of looking at things. By the end, you will have learned more about yourself. You may never start a business but I believe you will have a much more enterprising outlook on life and as a result, have a better life style.

I recently found a picture of me taken at the time when I was starting my first business. People I showed it to commented that I looked young and impressionable. And they were dead right. I was young, impressionable and idealistic. And if I'd had a book like Tortoise Walking For Beginners, I wouldn't have made so many silly mistakes. But then my loss is your gain. What can you learn from somebody who's had it easy and sailed effortlessly to the top? I made many misjudgements with regard to the type of business I should have started and the way of going about doing business.

But that's sorted now and I can honestly say I have never been more happy and comfortable in what I'm doing.

One of the real pleasures of my own personal tortoise walking journey has been meeting some wonderful people - and continuing to meet wonderful people. You don't know it yet but you'll discover for yourself that there are incredibly supportive people out there - including some fantastic bank managers! - who will be rooting for you and your enterprise. Of course, you're also going to meet the odd pillock on the way, but they're going to be outweighed by the people who have been there, done it and admire your enthusiasm and will help you get motivated again when you need it.

So go out there and get on with it, taking with you the words of entrepreneur and restaurateur, Bill Oldfield whose simple enterprise philosophy comprises three questions. He says: "I ask myself:

1. Have I satisfied the customer?
2. Have I made a profit in satisfying the customer.?
3. Have I had fun doing it?

If you can't answer 'yes' to all three questions, you should pack it in and start again."

THANK YOU

This book would never have happened had not the islanders of my first
ever Enterprise Island Challenge said: "Iain you have challenged us and
set us tasks. Now it's your turn. Where is the book?" So to Sarah, Alex,
Tim, Martyn, Jen, Lynn, John, Matt, Sandy, Wendy, Dean and Ange
thank you very much for forcing me to do
something I have been avoiding.

Of course there would never have been an Enterprise Island Challenge
in the first place had not Dave Smith of One North East backed it so
enthusiastically and had not Andy Hugman and Rural Enterprise
Tynedale and David McNight of Teesdale Market Towns Initiative
gone on to support a second and third Challenge.
Also immensely supportive have been Glyn Bateman and Roger Turner
at the Countryside Agency, so many thanks to them as well.

Before this turns into one of those rambling Academy Award speeches
thanks to everyone else out there...you know who you are, especially
Arthur Bell and David McGaan, who helped close one door
and open another.

However no man is an island (sorry) not even an Enterprise Island so a
very special thank you to Darren and Anita at Enterprise Island HQ.

And Finally.
We tried to do this book as an Enterprise Soap, as a
Cartoon book but without DeeDee Cuddihy this book
would still be my ramblings. Thank you DeeDee for
entertaining us, distracting us and inspiring us and for
turning my words into prose.